CARVERGUIDE 1

THE CHAIRPERSON'S ROLE AS SERVANT-LEADER TO THE BOARD

John Carver

Jossey-Bass Publishers
San Francisco

Manufactured in the United States of America.

Policy Governance℠ is a service mark of John Carver.

Library of Congress Cataloging-in-Publication Data

Carver, John.
    The chairperson's role as servant-leader to the board /
John Carver. — 1st ed.
       p. cm. — (CarverGuide ; 4)
     ISBN 0–7879–0300–0 (pbk.)
    1. Directors of corporations. 2. Corporate governance. 3. Chief
executive officers. I. Title. II. Series. III. Series: Carver, John.
The CarverGuide series on effective board governance ; 4.
HD2745.C372 1997
658.4'22—dc20   96-35715

PB Printing   10 9 8 7 6 5 4 3 2   FIRST EDITION

As the chairperson of the board, your role, on behalf of the board, is to protect and further the integrity of governance. This Carver-Guide helps you and your board develop your role as leader in this process, yet as servant to the board as a body. I have appropriated Robert Greenleaf's pithy term *servant-leader* because it captures the essence of your job so clearly.*

For you as chairperson to make the best contribution to your organization, it is important that your role and its relationship with the board and with the CEO be philosophically grounded in two points:

1. The seat of governance integrity begins with the board, not with the chairperson, as must the seat of governance authority. In short, we must formulate the board's job first, and only then derive the chairperson's role. In the board-chairperson dyad, the board must unambiguously be the superior, the chairperson the servant.

2. The chairperson, his or her role having been derived from—and therefore secondary to—the board's job, is charged to lead a process in which high-performance governance is the product. Although all board members bear a responsibility for

---

* From 1970 until his death in 1990, the late Robert K. Greenleaf wrote a series of essays and books beginning with *The Servant as Leader*. The most authoritative resource for continuing work in servant-leadership is the Robert K. Greenleaf Center, Indianapolis.

governance discipline, the chairperson as first-among-equals not only guides the process but is empowered to make certain decisions. As point-person for board discipline, the chairperson is the leader.

We must begin, then, by designing the board's job well. Once the board's role is clear, we can make sense of whatever parts it divides its labor into. Wholeness in the board's job is crucial. The board is a group, a single organizational position, not a collection of individuals or committees. Any division of board unity must be done judicially, because subdividing any whole endangers the wholeness. Board officers and committees, which are granted parts of the board's authority, are such subdivisions. Because the chairperson normally inherits the most visible and forceful of the board's subdivided roles, your role must be constituted with particular care. The purpose of your position is not to weaken the board's wholeness but to support and nurture it.

This CarverGuide will build on the points made above in this sequence. First, I explore governance process policies wherein the board outlines what it expects of itself. Then I discuss the fact that you, as chairperson, have specific responsibilities that are fundamental to the governance process and board discipline. I also discuss the roles of other officers. Then there are tips for you on becoming a more effective leader. Finally, I suggest a few characteristics to look for in your replacement, when that inevitable day comes for you to give up the job of chairperson.

Understanding Governance Process

How your board decides organizational results, how it controls operations, how it uses its time, what it gets involved with and leaves alone, and how it relates to staff reveal much about its job design. The best governance will result if the board deliberates and codifies how it will govern its own process (before governing the staff), including devising a job description by which to discipline time and activity. The board's perspectives on the governing task itself are assembled in the governance process category of policies.

Governance process policies are the policies in which your board of directors outlines its own role. This category begins with a very general overview statement of the board's purpose, its reason for existence, its own personal mission. The master policy in the governance process category might read like this:

> The board's job, on behalf of [identify the ownership here], is to see to it that [name of organization here] (1) achieves what it should and (2) avoids situations and conduct that are unacceptable.

Ownership is the population that owns the organization in a moral sense (and only sometimes in a legal sense). A city council's owners are residents of the city, while a trade association's owners are the association members. Other aspects of this statement will be addressed below.

The foregoing statement summarizes with a broad brush the entirety of a governing board's role and commitment. But I expect that your board will not be willing to leave the description of its own role and process to language as broad as this. Consequently, the board will want to go into further detail with its description. In Policy Governance, that means the board will define what it means by the original statement by going into the next lower level of policy.

While boards differ a lot in this regard, my experience is that boards often choose the following topics to be further delineated in additional board policies in this category:

- Board job products—an outcome or "value added" type of job description, one that details the "products" of the board itself
- Governing style—a description of the kind of process or manner in which the board will conduct its business
- Ownership linkage—the way in which the board will exercise its trusteeship in connecting with those who morally, if not legally, own the organization

- Planning cycle—a plan by which the board will get its job accomplished over a period of time, say, one year; this policy establishes the link between board job description and meeting agendas

- Agenda control—the manner in which specific agendas come together, as well as the method by which individual trustees can impact the agenda

- Officer roles—the authority and responsibility given to board officers, further specifying the skeletal description likely found in bylaws

- Code of conduct—what is expected of individual trustees in terms of conflict, participation, preparation, and general conduct

- Committee principles—the principles to be observed to avoid fragmentation of the board and confusion of the board's one-voice delegation to the CEO

- Committee structure—a listing of each committee of the board, along with the job product expected of each and the authority granted to each, such as authorization to use a specified amount of staff time or funds

Policies in this list are, as has been explained, further definitions of the "mega-policy" shown immediately before. Within each of these policies, the same level-by-level integrity is observed. For example, in each policy cited, a preamble would address the broadest matter. Your board would choose to go into more detail about that preamble only if it is unwilling to allow you, as chairperson, to make the further interpretation.

I must emphasize that the words in these policies are meant to be meant. That is, they are not intended to be verbal ornament but must be an ironclad commitment by the board to operate in a carefully crafted way. Traditional board practice is such that using words as meaningless decoration has been acceptable. If you are in doubt, read your own board documents closely, particularly the bylaws. Or look at unrealistic but rhetorically inspiring goal statements that imply an organization will serve everyone or will have no barriers to service. Unless the board treats its words in these policies as commitments, governing excellence will remain a pipe dream. Good governance relies heavily on the old adage, "Say what you mean, and mean what you say."

With governance process policies, your board makes its own practices explicit. When a board struggles with and ultimately defines its policies, there are a number of payoffs, some of which are evident only in the long term. But even short term, the board is stronger for having taken control of its own process. Because board members will not know what their own board intends unless its intentions are in writing, the process produces a welcome clarity for individual members. Because board policies—not you, the chairperson—are dominant, the risk of your becoming a runaway or dictatorial chairperson is small. (Of course, I am more worried about your successor than about you!) The board is less vulnerable to radical swings when it is time to pass your role of chairperson to a new person.

So the products and process of the board are recorded in the governance process category. However, you can see that while these policies give definition to the board's job, they do not describe the job in so much detail that every possible eventuality is answered. Thus it is sensible for the board to turn further decision making over to you.

Your Role in Governance Process

In the Policy Governance model, you, the chairperson, inherit the task of making smaller decisions about the board's job as events unfold. You have this authority, however, only as long as you act in a manner consistent with what the board has already stated.

Even without referring to Policy Governance, it's commonly accepted that the chair makes decisions and that these decisions should be true to the official decisions the board has already made.

However in Policy Governance, the board is much more explicit about how it will govern (governance process) and how it will connect to management (board-staff linkage). You are given considerable authority to make further decisions within the topics covered by governance process and board-staff linkage. Having these policies in written form will give you more confidence to take actions than you otherwise would have. Delegated authority is always easier to use when you know the ground rules up front.

Once the board has done its job of policy creation, you, in order to do your job, should be granted the right to use "any reasonable interpretation" of the board's words. Just as the board gives the CEO this same range of authority with respect to ends and executive limitations policies, it gives you this right with respect to governance process and board-staff linkage policies. After all, this right clarifies in what manner you can use your own judgment with respect to the board's words. Just like the CEO, you need clear enough authority so that you do not have to return to the board with the endlessly repeated entreaty, "Is this what you meant?" In other words, it is to the board's advantage to have a powerful but *bounded* chairperson.

Your abilities to make decisions within the boundaries of governance process and board-staff linkage extend beyond the organization to the public and the press. When interviewed, you have the authority to go beyond what the board has actually said, as long as you are doing so within a reasonable interpretation of what the board has said. Any board member can "represent the board" if that merely means stating only what the board has stated. This special authority of the chair, however, does not extend to ends and executive limitations policies, where the interpretation passes directly from the board to its CEO rather than to you.

To establish your boundaries as chairperson, it is important for your board to clearly define your role and to hold you accountable. You as chairperson inherit the opportunity to make decisions within the domain given you, but that carries the responsibility for performance. With respect to how the board has said it will behave, you will be evaluated on whether the board's words become reality.

For example, if the board says in policy that it will regularly evaluate its own performance, you have the right to interpret what "regularly" means. But it also means that you have the responsibility to see that such evaluation actually occurs. In fact, your *saying* that your interpretation of "regularly" is "quarterly" means little; what has meaning is that the *actual self-evaluations* are quarterly.

Your board should define its chairperson's role in a policy within the governance process category as illustrated in Exhibit 1. Remember that the content and the depth (the degree to which the policy language goes into narrower detail) shown in Exhibit 1 may not be best for your board. Every board must choose its own policy content and depth. The policy illustrated, however, is perfectly model-consistent. It is the model-consistency that should be constant, regardless of the particular board. In other words, if you have adopted a model, be sure to apply its principles consistently; otherwise, whatever power it can contribute to your governance will deteriorate.

Exhibit 1 illustrates that if the board creates policy about how its job is to be conducted, then you as chairperson can maintain good board behavior by basing your decisions on that policy. This is easier than invoking disciplinary measures on the basis of your individual sense of what should be. Not only will the board have assumed leadership about its own discipline (an important ingredient in developing group responsibility) but the resulting specific actions need not be invoked by you out of your own strength alone.

Chairperson's Role in Board Discipline

So it is the responsibility of the board as a whole, not your responsibility, to develop the initial rules of conduct so the board can stay disciplined and on track. The board says to itself, "We are a group, and groups always have a hard time with discipline. We know that. So what rules shall we have for ourselves so we will be a disciplined body in order to govern well?" With the rules set, the board turns to you and assigns the job of enforcing and even fleshing out the fine

Exhibit 1. Sample Board Policy: Chairperson's Job Description.

For continuity and discipline in government, the chairperson is charged to make decisions on issues of Governance Process and Board Staff Linkage within board policies.

1. The job result of the chairperson is that the board behaves consistently with its own rules and those legitimately imposed upon it from outside the organization.
   A. Meeting discussion content will only be those issues which, according to board policy, clearly belong to the board to decide, not the CEO.
   B. Deliberation will be fair, open, and thorough, but also efficient, timely, orderly, and kept to the point.

2. The authority of the chairperson consists in making decisions that fall within the topics covered by board policies on governance process and board staff linkage, except where the board specifically delegates portions of this authority to others. The chairperson is authorized to use any reasonable interpretation of the provisions in these policies.
   A. The chairperson is empowered to chair board meetings with all the commonly accepted power of that position (e.g. ruling, recognizing).
   B. The chairperson has no authority to make decisions about policies within ends and executive limitations policy areas. Therefore, the chairperson has no authority to supervise or direct the CEO.
   C. The chairperson may represent the board to outside parties on announcing board-stated positions and in stating chair decisions and interpretations within the area delegated to him or her.

Source: Carver, J. *Board Leadership: A Bimonthly Workshop with John Carver,* 1995, 17, p. 6.

points of board discipline. You are the point person for the board's commitment to discipline.

An interesting thing about your role is that the more your board is really responsible for doing its job as a body, with every board member being responsible for keeping the group on track, the less important it is for you to exercise discipline. Your experience and mine is that it makes a lot of difference who the chair is. But the reason it makes so much difference is that boards have not learned to be responsible as groups. To the extent that a group is *really* responsible as a group, who the chair is makes far less difference.

So, as the board sets out to fulfill its responsibilities, it first must deal with the implications of being a group. Indeed, this hurdle can easily keep a board from attending to other responsibilities. Boards are fraught with extensive interpersonal dynamics, as is any other group of human beings. I will look past the obvious psychological issues (since you have been chosen as the board's chair, not its therapist) to organizational features more susceptible to change.

Taking the time to design sound governance process policies is the board's greatest safeguard against the debilitating effects of unfortunate interpersonal dynamics. By carefully designing areas of board job performance, the board can profoundly channel the interpersonal process of a board. For example, a clear job performance design influences the types of conflict that will be experienced and the decision of members whether to follow a commonly proclaimed discipline or their individual disciplines. Job design also ensures that diversity is directed toward some areas and muted or eliminated in others. By clarifying tasks and off-limits topics through job design, your board helps to depersonalize subsequent struggles over the appropriateness of an issue for board discussion.

A sound, codified board job can ameliorate jockeying for power, control of the group through negativism, and diversion of the board into unrelated topics. As a result, dealing with the dysfunctional behavior of a board member and a poor interpersonal process is less difficult when the board has previously determined what constitutes appropriate behavior. Without board-developed guidelines, the matter will be considered a clash between personalities, and the issue of acceptable board behavior becomes lost in ill feelings.

As chairperson, you bear a peculiar responsibility with respect to the group aspect of governance process. More cogent to this discussion, however, the entire board cannot avoid its share of responsibility. In other words, your existence does not relieve other board members from contributing to the integrity of the process. If the board as a whole does not accept responsibility for governance process, the best you can achieve as chairperson is superficial discipline. Your board expects too much of you when they ask you to save them from being held hostage by the most controlling member or to be the only voice to ensure the group doesn't stray into unrelated topics or otherwise waste its time and compromise its carefully crafted process.

Other Board Officers

When the board's role and your responsibilities within that role are clear, then you and the board can pay attention to the need for additional officers. Commonly, boards establish the chairperson, vice chair, secretary, and treasurer, though it is not rare to find more than one vice chair and often a chair-elect.

Structure is best kept to the minimum necessary to accomplish the task. Establishment of more officers than needed increases complexity with no compensating gain. Consequently, your board should start with the minimum number of officers required by law and add more only as they are needed. In many jurisdictions, nonprofit boards can get by with two officers, chairperson and secretary.

From this minimalist standpoint, it is often hard to justify more officers. The office of vice chair usually exists only so that someone is readily available to fill in for an absent chairperson; however, a board can simply rotate temporary chairing duties in the absence of the chairperson. The board treasurer is an unnecessary office in any organization with a CEO. The CEO can, in many jurisdictions, double as secretary. The point I wish to make here, however, is not

which officers are justified but that establishment of the fewest officers called for by the task will result in clearer rules and process.

Remember that a successful board governs with one voice.
Consequently, board officers exist to help the board do its job, not
as powers unto themselves. Having a minimum number of officers
increases the chances for board holism. For the minimum two officer descriptions, I suggest the following job descriptions, stated in
the job product style:

Chairperson: Responsible for the integrity of the governing
process
Secretary: Responsible for the integrity of board documents

These job responsibilities serve the wholeness of governance. They
do not interfere with the board's unified delegation to the CEO.
Thus while you, as chairperson, are guardian of what the board
is doing, the secretary is guardian of what the board *has done*. If the
secretary's job product is "integrity of board documents," selection
of a secretary should be based on the ability to make that contribution. Responsible for no one else's behavior but his or her own, the
secretary need only be compulsive about correctness, accuracy, and
appearance. The secretary's job may have little to do with taking
minutes but will have much to do with the official record of process
and actions. He or she certifies the evidence of board action, including board policies and minutes.

Tips for Chairing Effectively

How you as a chairperson carry out your role has much to do with
the success of the board. A weak chair often fails to move a board
along and may be unable to prevent indecisiveness and the tendency to dance around issues. Strong chairs have been known to
run roughly over dissent and participation, but the point is not simply that you should be either retiring or strong. The point is that
you should lead individuals to become a *leadership group*. Members

should never assume that they can relax their group responsibility because you have saved them from it. Here are a few tips for chairing more effectively:

1. *Be the chairperson, not an intermittent CEO.* Do your own job. The board has already designated the top staff officer as chief executive. Your role is to help the board do a good job, not to run the organization. If your organization is too small to have a staff CEO, you may in fact have to perform both roles. If so, just be clear yourself and communicate clearly to others which hat you are wearing at any particular time. (Generally, in these tips, I will assume your organization has assigned the role of CEO to its top staff person.)

2. *Lead the board, not the CEO.* Your focus should be on the board, not on the staff. The CEO works for the board, not for you. Only the board has the right to tell the CEO what to do or to add to the board's criteria for judging CEO performance. An intermediary can only detract from crisp accountability. Consequently, don't worry about the CEO, worry about the board—that will be worry enough.

3. *Lead the board to define its own job.* Your purview is not to work your own agenda for the operating organization. Even your desire for better governance has to become the board's commitment before you can have much effect. Press the board to explore the ramifications of its moral (or sometimes legal) trusteeship and to define just what its job is. When the job is thus defined in its relatively permanent form, have the board set annual targets within segments of that job. This will help later as you set specific meeting agendas.

4. *Lead the board to design its discipline.* When you enforce the rules, it will be better if you are enforcing the board's rules, not yours. Help the board examine and plan its process—how the board will deal with dissent, with renegade members, with attendance, and with coming to meetings unprepared. Decisions about the rules the board chooses for itself should be written and adopted as board policy. Without group-determined discipline, there will either be insufficient discipline, or you will end up personally creating it.

5. *Lead the board to evaluate its performance.* Regularly return the board to what it adopted about its own job. Has it followed through?

Is it behaving the way it said it would? Be sure you stick to what the board has adopted as expectations and intentions for itself. Evaluations done apart from the job description are not as useful and may be a waste of time. Because it is easy for a board to slip back into old habits, I suggest that some self-evaluation be done every meeting.

6. *Take responsibility for the agenda.* This is the board's agenda, not the staff's—so don't leave the agenda to staff. The board's job is not to look over what the staff did last month or quarter but to get its own job done. If the board doesn't know about its own job more than staff does, then recognize that as a problem and go back to point 3 above. Developing agendas for specific meetings will be both easier and more board-empowering if the board as a body has engaged itself—even with a broad brush—in annual agenda planning.

7. *Run participative but efficient meetings.* Keep it open, but keep it moving! Encourage debate and differences; bring people out; make it acceptable to disagree. Create an atmosphere of respectful diversity. Yet do not allow the board to talk an issue to death. Using a simple poll—How many have your minds made up already?—can yield surprising and enlightening results. The informal polling technique, by the way, can be used to get quick readings from the board in many situations.

8. *Take the long view—build capability.* Efficient meetings are important, but don't put your emphasis on effective meetings per se. Focus on the long-term ability of the board to govern. You won't worry too much if a particular meeting is awkward and tedious if the board learns needed skills and insights from it or grapples meaningfully with an important value issue. Set out to leave the next chair with a board more in control of itself than you found it. The board will be less vulnerable to unhappy conditions thereafter, such as having a chairperson less wonderful than you are!

Passing the Torch

No chairperson stays in the position forever, and finding a replacement is an important part of governance process. The better the board, the more judiciously it chooses a chair (even though, as I've pointed out, the more responsible the board is as a group, the less your position makes a difference in the near term). Since your job product is integrity of the governing process, selection of your replacement should be based on ability to achieve that output. End forever the reckless tendency to choose a chairperson based on longevity, on who has the most time to spare, or as a reward. It is better to obtain a good leader who can invest three hours a month than a marginal leader who has thirty hours to give.

Your job requires skilled handling of group process, an ability to fairly but firmly lead a group to confront and even to welcome its diversity, and to adhere to agreed-upon rules for board conduct. Your board should take great care in choosing a replacement who can continue to develop the leadership that often lies dormant in the group. You and your board must realize that the good chair incites the board to generate all the rules it needs out of its own wisdom. Then you merely call forth the board's own statements of discipline when needed, as if you have no choice but to deal with the group the way the group itself has decreed.

Summary

Your role of chairperson comes as close to a pure instance of Robert Greenleaf's servant-leader as I can imagine. You are clearly the board's leader and just as surely its servant as well. Your job is not to lead the organization—it is the far more sensitive and demanding task of helping the board to lead the organization.

It is your responsibility to understand servant-leadership, understand governance process, and understand how a group of peers—all of whom bring diverse values—can be visionary, bold, and pragmatic all at the same time. Your job is as much about nurturance as about cracking the whip, as much about thorough deliberation as about decisiveness, and as much about stimulating diversity as about reaching a single, official decision. Your job is to encourage, cajole, pressure, and cheerlead your board to be all it can be.

The CarverGuide
Series on Effective
Board Governance

The Policy Governance model was created by John Carver in the mid 1970s as a radical alternative to the conventional wisdom about how governance should proceed. All governance literature at that time—and virtually all of it even today—was based on ideas about the board's role and responsibilities that had been around for a very long time.

Boards convinced that Policy Governance offers a breakthrough in governance thinking encounter a confusing problem: Most printed matter and training reinforce old governance ideas rather than the new ones. It is not that widely available sources do not have wisdom to offer. Indeed, they do. But the wisdom they have is rooted in traditional governance ideas. One of the great difficulties of a paradigm shift is that perfectly fine wisdom in a previous paradigm can become poor judgment in a new one. The person most expert in flying a propeller-driven plane is not, therefore, expert in piloting a jet.

Consequently, most current guides and training materials can actually handicap boards trying to use the new governance ideas in Policy Governance. The CarverGuide series has been created to remedy this situation. The series will offer detailed guidance on specific board responsibilities and operations based on the *new* paradigm rather than the traditional approach.

The first CarverGuide in the series presented an overview of the fundamental principles of the Policy Governance model. As a model, Policy Governance is designed to embrace all further issues of governance that are specific to different organizations and different circumstances. That is, it is not specifically about fiscal oversight, CEO evaluation, planning, agenda control, committee operation, or the other many facets of board leadership. It is, in fact, about all of them. It is a basic set of concepts and principles that lay the groundwork for determining appropriate board leadership about these and other common governance issues. Nonetheless, many boards need specific materials that individually do address these different facets of board leadership.

Having presented the overview in the first CarverGuide, we deal with the various areas of board concern one at a time in the succeeding guides in this series. It is our hope that the concepts and recommendations we present in this series will help all boards achieve a powerful overhaul of their approach to governance. Indeed, the practices we recommend in the CarverGuide Series really make sense only as parts of the larger picture of board leadership held up by the Policy Governance model.

Notes